Y0-CXM-054

Beverly Clark's

I Love You Because

Beverly Clark's

I Love You Because

Running Press

PHILADELPHIA · LONDON

Library of Congress Cataloging-in-Publication Number 98-68470

ISBN 0-7624-0626-7

This book may be ordered by mail from the publisher.
Please include $1.00 for postage and handling.
But try your bookstore first!

Running Press Book Publishers
125 South Twenty-second Street
Philadelphia, Pennsylvania 19103-4399

Visit us on the web!
www.runningpress.com

Contents

Introduction

Weddings make us cry. They are events infused with such joy that the participants are unable to keep themselves composed, weeping openly in public without considering how foolish or vulnerable they may appear. The lovers' vows are a promise of shared joy and lasting devotion that reaffirm our own vows or leave us longing to create ties of our own.

I love you because . . .

The answers are infinite. Each of us has our own reasons why we are drawn to each other. We rarely know what specific traits in another person make us love them. No matter how hard we try, we are unable to sufficiently put into words why we love each other. It's like trying to explain why we breathe. We just do.

Love nourishes us, strengthening our hearts and souls and helping us to grow. While we may feel love differently, we are all changed by its presence in our lives. In my previous book, *Weddings: A Celebration*, we celebrated the different ways people express their love on this most romantic of occasions. A wedding is a day for sharing love, happiness and traditions with the ones closest to you. It is an open declaration of our love for each other and a promise that we will always be together.

In marriage, we give a beloved part of ourselves. It is the union of two hearts, two people, and two lives. This day, when we pledge ourselves forever to one person, is truly a cause for celebration.

With This Ring,
I Thee Wed

We looked into each
other's eyes. I saw myself,
she saw herself.

Stanislaw J. Lec (1909–1966)
Polish writer

Until I met my husband,
I didn't believe in love
at first sight.
But an hour after I met him,
before I'd kissed him,
I knew I'd marry him.

Ricki Lake
American talk-show host

It is the man and woman
united that make the
complete human being.
Together, they are most likely
to succeed in the world.

Benjamin Franklin (1706–1790)
American writer and statesman

In love,
all of life's contradictions
dissolve and disappear.
Only in love are unity and
duality not in conflict.

Rabindranath Tagore (1861–1941)
Bengali poet and mystic

BOTH OF US ARE VERY SPLASHY
VIVID PICTURES, THOSE KIND
WITH THE DETAILS LEFT OUT,
BUT I KNOW THAT OUR COLORS
WILL BLEND. . . .

Zelda Sayre Fitzgerald (1900 – 1948)
American writer

*What made me love her? . . .
the words that I might call upon
to explain my condition are
insufficient, so pathetic, that in
the end the best, truest
words I can offer . . . are these
three: I don't know.*

Andrew Postman
American writer

*L*ove you?
I am you.

Charles Williams (1886–1945)
English writer

Perfect truth, perfect honesty, perfect candor, were qualities of my wife's character which were born with her. . . . I have compared and contrasted her with hundreds of persons and my conviction remains that hers was the most perfect character I have ever met.

Mark Twain (1835–1910)
American writer

*And indeed I felt happy
with her, so perfectly happy, that
the one desire of my mind was
that it should differ in nothing
from hers, and already I wished
for nothing beyond her smile,
and to walk with her thus, hand
in hand, along a sun-warmed,
flower-bordered path.*

André Gide (1869–1951)
French writer

. . . is there anything on earth or heaven that would have made me so happy as to have made you mine long ago? And not less now than then, but more than ever at this time. You know that I would with pleasure give up all here and all beyond the grave for you. . . .

I was and am yours freely and most entirely, to obey, to honor, [to] love and fly with you when, where, and how you yourself might and may determine.

George Gordon, Lord Byron
(1788–1824) English poet

WHEN YOU REALIZE YOU
WANT TO SPEND THE REST OF
YOUR LIFE WITH SOMEONE,
YOU WANT THE REST OF YOUR
LIFE TO START AS SOON
AS POSSIBLE.

Nora Ephron (b. 1941)
American writer

. . . there is a gleam of the magic circle on my finger that warms my heart with its more than precious message from you. At night I usually take off my rings but this one will stay where I can feel it, even in my dreams.

Edith Bolling Galt Wilson (1872–1961)
American First Lady

*H*ear the mellow wedding
bells, Golden bells!
What a world of happiness
their harmony foretells!

Edgar Allan Poe (1800–1849)
American writer

*A good marriage is at least
eighty percent good luck in
finding the right person at
the right time. The rest is trust.*

Nanette Newman
British actress

$\mathcal{M}$y most brilliant
achievement was my ability
to persuade my wife to
marry me.

Winston Churchill (1874–1965)
British Prime Minister

Seeing you as I saw you last night, my radiant, wonderful Darling, is like witnessing some deep and glorious mystery, like being present while life is created. There are moments when I feel the awe of it and wonder why I was permitted to be the instrument of it. And the beauty and joy of it is unspeakable. I love you with an intensity that hurts me because it can have no adequate expression.

Woodrow Wilson (1856–1924)
American President

In marriage do thou be wise:
prefer the person before
money, virtue before beauty,
the mind before the body;
then thou hast
a wife, a friend, a companion,
a second self.

William Penn (1644–1718)
English statesman

THERE IS NO MORE FRIENDLY
AND CHARMING RELATIONSHIP,
COMMUNION, OR COMPANY THAN
A GOOD MARRIAGE.

Martin Luther (1483–1546)
German religious reformer

. . . the unit of the wife and
husband begins as a fresh
creation, as innocent and full of
promise as any newborn.

Arlene Hamilton Stewart
American writer

Alas, that my heart is a lute,
Whereon you have
learned to play!
For many years it was mute,
Until one summer's day
You took it, and touched it,
and made it thrill
And it thrills and throbs,
and quivers still!

Anne Lindsay (1750–1825)
English poet

What greater thing is there for two human souls than to feel that they are joined . . . to strengthen each other . . . [and] to be one with each other in silent unspeakable memories.

George Eliot [Mary Ann Evans]
(1819–1880) English writer

*T*here is nothing
nobler or more admirable
than when two people who
see eye to eye keep house
as man and wife . . .

Homer (Ninth-Century B.C.)

To Love, Honor, and Cherish

*L*ove is not a decision
your brain makes. It's a
feeling you know somewhere
else, and your brain catches
up. . . . But love challenges
you in areas you need to be
challenged in. It rests
somewhere in not knowing
what's going to happen.
Not predicting.

Meg Ryan (b. 1962)
American actress

*What is love? . . .
It is the morning and the
evening star.*

Sinclair Lewis (1885–1951)
American writer

A coward is incapable of exhibiting love; it is the prerogative of the brave.

Mohandas K. Gandhi (1869–1948)
Indian nationalist

To love is also good, for love is difficult. For one human being to love another is perhaps the most difficult task of all, the epitome, the ultimate test. It is the striving for which all other striving is merely preparation.

Ranier Maria Rilke (1875–1926)
German poet

Love is the heart's immortal thirst to be completely known and all forgiven.

Henry Van Dyke (1852–1933)
American poet and writer

Why did I love her?
Because it was her;
because it was me.

Michel Eyquem de Montaigne
(1533–1592)
French writer

THERE IS ONLY ONE TERMINAL DIGNITY IN LOVE. AND THE STORY OF A LOVE IS NOT IMPORTANT, WHAT IS IMPORTANT IS THAT ONE IS CAPABLE OF LOVE. IT IS PERHAPS THE ONLY GLIMPSE WE ARE PERMITTED OF ETERNITY.

Helen Hayes (1900–1993)
American actress

To love and to cherish, it was always music in my ears, both before and after our marriage, when my husband told me that I was the only one he had ever thought of, or cared for...

Mary Todd Lincoln (1818–1882)
American First Lady

We never live so intensely
as when we love strongly. We
never realize ourselves so
vividly as when we are in full
glow of love for others.

Walter Rauschenbusch (1861–1918)
American theologian

In our life there
is a single color, as on an
artist's palette, which provides
the meaning of life and art.
It is the color of love.

Marc Chagall (1887–1985)
Russian-born French artist

*Love is a portion of the
soul itself, and it is the
celestial breathing of the
atmosphere of paradise.*

Victor Hugo (1802–1884)
French writer

A WISE LOVER VALUES NOT SO
MUCH THE GIFT OF THE LOVER
AS THE LOVE OF THE GIVER.

Thomas á Kempis (c.1379 – 1471)
Dutch theologian

Love gives us in a moment
what we can hardly attain by
effort after years of toil.

Johann Wolfgang von Goethe (1747–1812)
German writer

To love someone
is to see a miracle
invisible to others.

Francois Mauriac (1885–1970)
French writer

*When one has once fully
entered the realm of love,
the world—no matter how
imperfect—becomes rich and
beautiful, it consists solely of
opportunities for love.*

Søren Kierkegaard (1813–1855)
Danish philosopher and critic

LOVE IS THE TRUE MEANS BY
WHICH THE WORLD IS ENJOYED.

Thomas Traherne (1637–1674)
American clergyman and poet

I am certain of nothing
but the holiness of the
heart's affections . . .

John Keats (1795–1821)
English poet

LOVE IS FRIENDSHIP
SET ON FIRE.

Jeremy Taylor (1613–1667)
English clergyman and writer

There is no place
like a bed for confidential
disclosures between friends.
Man and wife, they say,
there open the very bottom of
their souls to each other, and
some old couples often lie
and chat over old times till
nearly morning.

Herman Melville (1819–1801)
American writer

*The intense happiness of
our union is derived from the
perfect freedom with which
we each follow and declare our
own impressions.*

George Eliot [Mary Ann Evans]
(1819–1880)
English writer

LOVE ENABLES TWO
PEOPLE TO GROW INTO
THEIR SENSE OF "WE," BUT NOT
AT THE EXPENSE OF THEIR
SENSE OF "I."

Dwight Small
American writer

The human heart, at whatever
age, opens only to the heart
that opens in return.

Maria Edgeworth (1767–1849)
British writer

Love is a taste of paradise.

Sholom Aleichem (1859–1916)
Yiddish writer

*To love one who loves you,
to admire one who admires
you, in a word, to be the idol
of one's idol, is exceeding the
limit of human joy; it is
stealing fire from heaven.*

Delphine de Girardin (1804–1855)
French writer

LOVE . . . MAY BE YOUR
GLIMPSE OF TRANSCENDENCE.

Florida Scott-Maxwell (1883 – 1978)
English psychologist

In Sickness
and in Health

My life is a very, very happy one.
It's a happiness of being
connected, of knowing that there
is someone I trust completely,
and that the one I trust is
the one I love.

Bill Cosby (b. 1937)
American entertainer and writer

The most precious gift that marriage gave me was this constant impact of something very close and intimate yet all the time unmistakably other, resistant—in a word, real.

C. S. Lewis (1898–1963)
English writer

To be rooted is perhaps
the most important and
least recognized need of
the human soul.

Simone Weil (1909–1943)
French social philosopher and activist

It is a lovely thing to have husband and wife developing together. That is what a marriage really means: helping one another to reach the full status of being persons, responsible and autonomous beings who do not run away from life.

Paul Tounier
American writer

People are like vines. . . .
We are born and we grow.
Like vines, people also need a
tree to cling to, to give
them support.

Elizabeth Kata
Australian writer

MARRIAGE IS A PARTNERSHIP
IN WHICH EACH INSPIRES
THE OTHER, AND BRINGS
FRUITION TO BOTH.

Millicent Carey McIntosh
American writer

Charles is life itself—pure life force, like sunlight—and it is for this that I married him and this is what holds me to him—caring always, caring desperately what happens to him and whatever he happens to be involved in.

Anne Morrow Lindbergh (b. 1906)
American writer and aviator

The bonds of matrimony are like any other bonds—they mature slowly.

Peter De Vries (1910–1993)
American writer

To keep your marriage
brimming,

With love in the loving cup,

Whenever you're wrong,
admit it;

Whenever you're right,
shut up.

Ogden Nash (1902–1971)
American poet

The best part of married
life is the fights.
The rest is merely so-so.

Thornton Wilder (1897–1975)
American playwright

THE GREAT SECRET OF A
SUCCESSFUL MARRIAGE IS TO
TREAT ALL DISASTERS AS
INCIDENTS AND NONE OF THE
INCIDENTS AS DISASTERS.

Harold Nicholson (1886–1968)
British diplomat and writer

*M*arriage is not just
communion and passionate
embraces; marriage is also
three meals a day, sharing the
workload, and remembering
to take out the trash.

Joyce Brothers (b. 1925)
American psychologist

A successful marriage is an edifice that must be rebuilt every day.

André Maurois (1885–1967)
French writer

THIS IS MY PLEDGE,
DEAREST ONE, I WILL STAND BY
YOU . . . AND NO MATTER
WHETHER THE WINE BE BITTER
OR SWEET WE WILL SHARE IT
TOGETHER AND FIND HAPPINESS
IN THE COMRADESHIP.

Edith Bolling Galt Wilson (1872–1961)
American First Lady

Unconditional love not only means I am with you, but also I am for you, all the way, right or wrong. . . . Love is indescribable and unconditional.

Duke Ellington (1899–1975)
American jazz musician

*I*n the consciousness
of belonging together, in
the sense of constancy,
resides the sanctity, the beauty
of matrimony, which helps
us to endure pain more easily,
to enjoy happiness doubly,
and to give rise to the fullest
and finest development of
our nature.

Fanny Lewald (1811–1889)
German writer

I AM YOUR LAUGHTER AND
YOU ARE MINE!

Eugene O'Neill (1888–1953)
American playwright

I shall not attempt to tell you what she is to me. Her entire sweetness of temper makes it a delight to breathe the same air with her—and I cannot imagine any condition of life, however full of hardship, which her presence would not render not merely supportable but delicious. It is nothing to me that my whole life shall be devoted to such a woman—its only happiness will consist in such a devotion.

Robert Browning (1812–1889)
English poet

I am most immoderately
married:
The Lord God has taken
my heaviness away; . . .
Being, not doing,
is my first joy.

Theodore Roethke (1908–1963)
American poet

Love keeps the cold out
better than a cloak.
It is food and raiment.

Henry Wadsworth Longfellow
(1807–1882)
American poet

*Till Death
Do Us Part*

She has been the
unspoken half of everything
I ever wrote, and both halves
of many a thing. . . .

Robert Frost (1874—1963)
American poet

He'd touched her on a level no one else ever had. Perhaps it was because when they'd looked at each other the first time, they'd also looked down the road. And what they'd seen, they'd seen together, as if there would never be a time when they would part.

Allan Folsom
American writer

LOVE DOES NOT CONSIST IN
GAZING AT EACH OTHER BUT IN
LOOKING OUTWARD TOGETHER
IN THE SAME DIRECTION.

Antoine de Saint-Éxupéry (1900–1944)
French aviator and writer

Throughout our years together,
we had built up a history and
a closeness so subtle we didn't
even know it was there.

Erma Bombeck (1923–1996)
American writer

*Chains do not hold
a marriage together. It is
threads, hundreds of tiny
threads which sew people
together through the years.
That is what makes a
marriage last. . . .*

Simone Signoret (b. 1921)
French actress

The love we have in our youth
is superficial compared to that
an old man has for his old wife.

Will Durant (1885–1981)
American writer

*Heaven will be no heaven
to me if I do not meet
my wife there.*

Andrew Jackson (1767–1845)
American President

I am yours, you are mine, of that be sure. You are locked in my heart, the little key is lost and now you must stay there forever.

Alexandra (1872–1918)
Czarina of Russia

And do you feel and know,
that as for me . . . for my
position as a wife . . . it is
awfully happy for this world.
He is too good and tender,
and beyond me in all things,
and we love each other with a
love that grows instead of
diminishing.

Elizabeth Barrett Browning (1806–1861)
English poet

You can see them alongside
the shuffleboard course in Florida
or on the porches . . . up north.
They are in love, they have always
been in love, although sometimes
they would have denied it. And
because they have been in love
they have survived everything that
life could throw at them.

Ernest Havemann (b. 1912)
American Writer

A marriage is a symphony with changes in mood and tempo, intricate little counterpoints, and re-echoings of earlier themes. The symphony is disciplined and may at first sound restrained, but you can play it again and again, and each time you'll hear a new bit of beauty you hadn't noticed before.

Linda Henly (b. 1951)
American writer

*I*f I had to live my life
over again, I don't think I'd
change it in any particular of
the slightest consequence.
I'd choose the same parents,
the same birthplace,
the same wife.

H. L. Mencken (1880–1956)
American writer

A MARRIAGE BETWEEN MATURE
PEOPLE IS NOT AN ESCAPE BUT
A COMMITMENT SHARED BY TWO
PEOPLE THAT BECOMES PART
OF THEIR COMMITMENT TO
THEMSELVES AND SOCIETY.

Betty Friedan (b. 1921)
American writer

Two such as you with
such a master speed
Cannot be parted nor
be swept away
From one another once
you are agreed
That life is only life
forevermore
Together wing to wing
and oar to oar.

Robert Frost (1874–1963)
American poet

Love is an act of endless
forgiveness, a tender look
which becomes a habit.

Peter Ustinov (b. 1921)
English actor and writer

A successful marriage requires
falling in love many times,
always with the same person.

Mignon McLaughlin
American writer and editor

*T*o keep the fire burning
brightly there's one easy rule:
Keep the two logs together,
near enough to keep each
other warm and far enough
apart—about a finger's
breath—for breathing room.

Marnie Reed Crowell
American writer

LOVE DEEPENS AND GROWS
WITH EVERY PASSING YEAR. . . .
SAYING "I DO" WAS MERELY
THE START OF A BEAUTIFUL
RELATIONSHIP.

Lynne Dumas
American writer

The sum which two married people owe to one another defies calculation. It is an infinite debt, which can only be discharged through all eternity.

Johann Wolfgang von Goethe
(1747–1812)
German writer

Sensual pleasure passes and vanishes in the blink of an eye, but the friendship between us, the mutual confidence, the delights of the heart, the enchantment of the soul, these things do not perish and can never be destroyed. I shall love you until I die.

Voltaire (1694–1778)
French writer

A husband,
a good marriage,
is earth.

Anne Morrow Lindbergh (b. 1906)
American writer and aviator

Photography Credits

Adams & Faith Photography: p. 101

Clay Blackmore: pp. 51, 75

Sidney Cooper: p. 56

Peter Diggs: p. 23

Chuck Gardner Photography: p. 87

Michael Garland: pp. 44, 126

G. Gregory Geiger: p. 123

Stephanie Hogue: p. 92

Brain Kramer: p. 21

Claudia Kunin: p. 72

Fred Marcus: p. 39

Heidi Mauracher: p. 80

Scott A. Nelson: title page, pp. 6, 15

Joann Pecdraro: p. 10

Durango Steele: pp. 29, 34, 40, 63, 68, 98, 106, 113, 118

This book has been bound using handcraft methods, and is Smyth-sewn to ensure durability.

The dust jacket and interior were designed by Toni Renée Leslie.

The text was edited by Elaine M. Bucher.

The text was set in Bernhard Modern, Nuptial Script, and Optima.